Steps to Online Dating Success

"Your Fun-Filled Guide to Match-Making the Online Dating Way in 5 Simple Steps!"

LEGAL NOTICE

The Publisher has strived to be as accurate and complete as possible in the creation of this report, notwithstanding the fact that he does not warrant or represent at any time that the contents within are accurate due to the rapidly changing nature of the Internet.

While all attempts have been made to verify information provided in this publication, the Publisher assumes no responsibility for errors, omissions, or contrary interpretation of the subject matter herein. Any perceived slights of specific persons, peoples, or organizations are unintentional.

In practical advice books, like anything else in life, there are no guarantees of income made. Readers are cautioned to reply on their own judgment about their individual circumstances to act accordingly.

This book is not intended for use as a source of legal, business, accounting or financial advice. All readers are advised to seek services of competent professionals in legal, business, accounting, and finance field.

You are encouraged to print this book for easy reading.

Table of Contents

What You Need to Know About Online Dating… First!	5
What Makes Online Dating So Different?	7
Step 1: Getting Started	13
Step 2: Making Yourself Look Like A Million Dollars	19
Step 3: Letting The Relationship Blossom	28
Step 4: Meeting Face To Face	32
Step 5: Once Bitten…	38
In Closing	39
Recommended Resources + Bonuses	40

Steps to Online Dating Success

What You Need to Know About Online Dating... First!

Online dating is not all fun and games and there are a lot of things that a person has to know about online dating before one gets into the intricacies of it. Online dating may seem to be the simplest thing in the world but it is not. It should be viewed in all earnestness or things could go haywire. Every game has its rules and unless you know all the rules you just can't become a good player and eventually a winner.

Tastes Differ

There are so many kinds of people around. Just look around you, how many people you know look the same?

Sizes, builds, shapes, features... they are all so different.

And that is just about the external appearances. And when it comes to character, it becomes a very different story altogether. Take a trip down memory lane, go back to your classrooms and take a look around.

A classroom is one place where we get to interact with a lot of different people on a very close basis. We get to rub shoulders and corners with very different people and we get to know them on a one to one basis. So how many of your classmates did you genuinely like?

I don't mean like them as classmates but as people. Was it easy to get along with all of them? That is why we often end up with best friends or clichés in classrooms.

We do not and do not have to like every body. The tastes and interests of one person might match with ours while the tastes and interests of another person may be at complete loggerheads with ours.

So when it comes to dating, it is very much the same story. But over here there are some strings attached. Unlike in a classroom contact, most people go on dates with a more impressive purpose, and that is to find life mate. There are a hundred and one things that should match before two people decide to spend the rest of their lives with each other.

Many people are of the opinion that they do not need any help with dating. They may be right because no body knows a person's tastes and likes better than the person himself or herself.

Maybe most of us do not need any help in making the right choice but **isn't it good to get a few pointers on the dating process as such, particularly on Online dating**? It is with this objective that this matter was prepared so that the thousands who are now availing of Internet dating may get the best out of it.

Reading This E-Book

I understand that most of my readers are very busy people who do not have too much time to spend reading an instruction manual.

So I have come up with something that requires just a single glance to get the gist of it. At the most you might require 10-15 minutes to run your eyes along the entire length of this book. It's that simple. But at the same time, do not let the simplicity mislead you. It is indeed a very comprehensive work that aims to leave no stones unturned.

You can either use this book as a general guideline to streamline your match-hunting venture, or you can keep coming back to it to make sure of every step before you actually put your foot forward. I can promise you that if you use this book to guide you, there is *no need to fear at all…you just won't stumble*.

What Makes Online Dating So Different?

We, human beings have been in this world for so many thousands of years. And since the beginning people have been choosing partners. Cultures across the world are very different and we can come across so many different ways in which people choose their life mates.

But the concept of finding a life partner with the help of the Internet is a fairly recent concept when compared with the history of mankind as such. Of course the Internet and computers have influenced man's life so much that it is no surprise that in the matters of finding a suitable partner too, the Internet has made its presence felt.

Online dating is, to put is very simply or flatly, finding a partner with the help of a machine namely the computer via the Internet. That itself makes the idea and the process a very novel one indeed, Hundreds of happy people across the globe have been successful in finding suitable partners by the means of online dating.

But to be frank with you, a lot of not-so-lucky persons have been goofed and jilted by the same process. So in order to make sure that you find a place in the first list let us go into the details of Online dating.

The Magic of the Internet

Everything that applies to the Internet, applies to Online dating as well. The Internet as we know allows for unlimited possibilities in communication, and it is this feature that has proved to be at the same time the biggest boon, as well as bane for Online dating.

People can start from scratch and get to know everything about each other before the actual meeting takes place. Tastes and preferences, likes and dislikes, interests and obsessions can be discussed on a one to one basis so that when the meeting actually takes place these two people are not in the least strangers to each other. Wonderful, isn't it?

But at the same time this possibility for unlimited communication leaves a lot of space for guile as well. The human race is endowed with a remarkable ability to use, misuse and abuse the same thing. And naturally, Online dating too has been and is still being used for vile purposes.

The person who is misusing this facility may either be a practical joker or may be someone with more devious intentions who is out to get some victims. It is because of this reason that a little bit of homework is good before you actually hit the road.

But you do not have to worry, the home work has already been painstakingly done for you and all you have to do is run your eyes along the following lines and you will be all set to strike gold.

How Did Online Dating Become So Popular?

The reason is *pretty simple*. It is very much the same reason that the Internet itself became so popular. The Internet opens up a whole new world of communication and contact. And the reasons for this are given below.

- **Speed**

    Try to picture what used to happen earlier in the days when people had to depend on the good ol' postal system. During those days, a person had to wait for one or two days for a letter to get across to a person who lived in the same state itself. The second person in turn would take one or two days to respond and this letter would take on or two days to get back to the first person.

    So in effect, a single correspondence would stretch over a week. But now it's a totally different story. The time taken for the first letter and the response has been brought to an amazing 2 minutes!

    Waiting may make the heart grow fonder but e-mail makes two people get close faster!

- **Privacy**

    The Internet provides for absolute privacy too. One can carry out communication with another person in the absolute privacy of one's bedroom or bath room or wherever one chooses to be. There is no fear of eavesdropping (ugh) or over hearing (shudder!) thanks to e-mail and chat facilities.

- **Options and Opportunities**

    The Internet provides for other options like voice chat or video conferencing and stops short only of the physical touch. But then who would want to start a relationship by touching right away?

You can see a person, talk to a person, and listen to the person's voice, can you think of a better way to start a date?

- **Economy**

    All this and more it is possible thanks to the Internet and the best part is that all this comes to you for peanuts. All you need is a PC (*who doesn't have one?*) and an Internet Connection (*how can anybody live without one?*) and you are all set. The only thing more you could ask for is a step-by-step guide to find your dream date…well here it is!

    So what are we waiting for?

Be Clear About What You Want

We all know that man is a social being. However man is also a lonely being. (And when we say man, we mean women too). Man longs for company.

Company not just from friends and the family, but from that special person with whom he or she can share those sweet nothings, those simple pleasures and pains, someone with whom he or she can build a whole new life, someone with whom he or she can raise a family of his or her own.

Now this is a fundamental need of man: **to find a life mate**. And the most popular method used for this is dating. When we talk about dating in the very finest sense of the word, please understand that dating is not to be viewed as a precursor for sleeping together. It is much more than that. It is the first step towards choosing a life partner and online dating has made the whole process a lot simpler now.

Marriage Versus A Casual Relationship

Now what you do and what you want is entirely your business. I don't want to sound nosey but I would like to draw a fine line between the kind of dating that is involved in these two quests.

Of course we are all grown up and so let us act like grown ups. Obviously in a casual relationship we are looking for fun. And mind you, fun can have a lot of connotations. So **here the object of one's desire will obviously be a person who is not inclined towards a serious relationship.**

If both parties are of the same view then it is well and good because they understand each other perfectly and do not expect much from such a relationship. This leaves no room for heartbreak.

It is when one party is in for something more serious and the other party is into sheer frivolousness that the problems start. So you should be absolutely clear about what you are looking for from the start, and you should make your intentions very clear to the other person.

At the same time you should have no doubts about the intentions of the other person as well. Remember, even if it is a casual relationship, there should be mutual understanding at least about the nature of the relationship.

Of course, there is yet another possibility where a casual relationship can blossom into something more serious. But, again in such cases it is your instincts that can help you identify what is good and what is bad.

No matter how strong a person is, anyone can be taken for a ride or be taken for granted. Being jilted is never a nice experience. So those of you who are going in for a casual relationship, for heavens sake, be on your guard! Marriage is altogether a different story but we will deal with that later.

Dating Comes From a Fundamental Need

Let's face it, of course sex is important, but sex is by far **NOT** the most important reason for dating.

Important! Maybe during the age of thoughtless youth, when new hormones are being pumped in and out, **sex is on every one's mind. But as one matures** (mind you that does not mean growing old and gray) sex takes the back seat and mutual support, likes and dislikes, cooperation, caring and sharing come to the forefront. We start thinking about building up a world of our own and we need someone to share it with, and not just someone to sleep with.

Sex is a fundamental need of every human being. We all have it in us to give and receive physical pleasure. But when you sit and think about it for a minute, you can see that this urge is actually the result of another urge.

There is a more primary urge in every human being to breed and produce offspring, and it is this urge that gives rise to such a powerful sexual desire. But whatever be the urge, the most dignified means to satisfy it is dating.

Nobody, not one of us, is complete without a partner; and it is to satisfy this need that people date. Because of this, the rest of this manual will be dedicated not to finding the right sex partner, but to finding the right life partner.

Online Dating Is Here To Stay

Let's accept the fact that dating couldn't really get better. **Online dating is THE real thing.** Let's compare it to the old system of evening balls or social gatherings. Imagine you are this big gathering where there are a lot of men and women looking out for suitable partners.

Suppose you bump into one or two people with whom you seem to strike an immediate rapport. You are then able to take this person out onto a balcony with just the moon to keep an eye on you.

You get to talk to this person for hours and hours; just talk and nothing else. You get to discuss likes and dislikes and finally when it is time to part you leave with a promise to meet on a following day at an equally enjoyable spot. These talks go on for days and weeks and finally you decide that this indeed is the THE person with whom you want to spend the rest of your life with.

Then of course you start meeting in more open places, you hold hands and even kiss. You begin to go out for lunch and dinner and spend even more intimate time together. When the moment is right and your decision is made, it then becomes time for you to say, "*I do.*"

Sigh! It sounds like a nice fairy tale, doesn't it?

Well it needn't be. It could be your own love story because the concept of online dating is just what has been described above. If you click the right buttons everything could work out fine for you and we have evidence to prove it. Just take a look at the figures given below and you can behold for yourself what a universal phenomenon online dating has already become.

As I mentioned earlier, one of the best things about online dating is that it affords a lot of privacy. You can chat for hours, video conference, or do whatever it is you care to do without arousing the interest of others or attracting the wrong kind of attention. All you need is a computer and Internet access everything becomes as discreet as can be. But along with that, may I add that we need a little bit of common sense as well or else we might find ourselves within the clutches of many lurid monsters lurking out there.

Another good thing about online dating is that it saves a lot of money which otherwise you would have had to splurge each time you took someone out on a date. It is because of these reasons and many more personal reasons that thousands of people find online dating to be a great convenience.

How To Get The Most Out Of Online Dating

Many people who decide to give online dating a try often end up with their hair singed and fingers burnt.

The reason we decided to put together such a manual is that online dating is not as simple as it looks. You need to know how to go about it in order to get the best out of it. Most people do not like to take chances and when it comes to finding a life partner people do not want to take chances at all.

But you can relax for through this manual we will be dealing with all the do's and the don'ts and so the whole process will be quite easy and enjoyable to you. This manual will provide you with step-by-step instructions on how to being online dating.

We have no doubts about the decision-making abilities of our readers and so we do not propose to give a lot of advice on the issue. Our purpose is simply to provide a couple of guidelines which we hope our readers will find valuable as they proceed in the attempt to find the perfect partner.

Step 1: Getting Started

Only fools rush in where angels fear to tread.

It is always best to approach unfamiliar territory with caution. You need to plan before you actually go out there and start dealing your cards. Be sure about yourself and be sure about what you want. Just because anyone and everyone can type out whatever they want in a chat room doesn't mean that we have to do the same.

The Internet has a wonderful quality of being accessible to every one. But this same quality attracts all kinds of people into it. But just because a lot of people who enter a chat room have only dirt on their minds, it doesn't mean that everyone is like that. If you stick to the class that you have and maintain your poise, you can indeed get the right kind of response.

There are a lot of nice people using the Internet, but it all depends on what you do. Do onto others what you want them to do to you is the golden rule that applies here. There are no rules for the game. All are players out there. But just because others are ruffians, it doesn't mean that you have to be one too. Your approach is the only thing that can get you the kind of response that you want.

I don't think that it is very sensible to decide all of the sudden that you would like to use the Internet to get a date. By just entering a chat room and saying "I'm available" you are merely putting yourself up for sale, and will most likely not get the results you desire.

One point that all of us have to understand is that in a chat room, all are equal. Do not go by the misconception that entering a chat room is like sauntering into a ball room dressed in your best. Then everyone turns to stare at you and the most eligible person (read that as the sexiest person of the opposite sex) catches your eye and makes his or her way towards you.

That kind of thing happens only on James Bond movies and we all know that James Bond never goes in for a serious relationship. It's all fun and games for him.

Where Do You Start?

The first tip we would like to give you is **NOT to go straight away into a singles' chat** room and try to find somebody who would interest you. All of us know that most of such chat rooms are virtually flooded with people who have only one thing on their mind - sex.

So, no matter what you ask for, it always ends up in that and the purpose is defeated. You will never get the kind of person who kind of matches your interests and tastes.

Sometimes it can really get quite infuriating. Everything starts off well. You are having a nice conversation with a person and warming up when all of the sudden, the topic moves towards the three letter word. The you let out a sigh and either have to bar messages from that person and risk the person bad mouthing you in a public chat room. Usually you have to leave the chat room all together.

In other words, **it is the easiest thing to get someone to sleep with you but if you are looking for something more enduring, like a partner for life, then you are going to have to be a little more patient**. The pick of the litter is not easy to find. But you do find it; it is going to be worth the effort.

So instead of going into a singles' chat room, what you could do is, you could try the whole thing out from a different angle. You could try working backwards.

More Than Looks

Sit for a minute or two and try and think about the things that interest you and things that you would find interesting in a person.

By 'things' over here I am not referring to physical attributes. I am not referring to something that might interest you in a person's physical appearance. Again the distinction has to be drawn between a serious relationship and a casual relationship. In a casual relationship, the importance is always for the physical attributes. We are more concerned with what the person looks like and what the person has been endowed with.

On the other hand, if we have a serious relationship, then the physical qualities are not so important. Compatibility is probably the most important factor over here. Along with that there are certain qualities that obviously we will be looking out for. We are talking about qualities of the mind. After all, beauty is only skin-deep!

This idea might sound strange, but it is actually true. The idea is that it is possible to grow to like the looks of a person. Once you find the character of the person agreeable you will start liking the person as a whole. It is entirely possible to fall in love with a person if the person does not look like a movie star. That is one of the tricks that nature plays.

There are many people who insist on taking a look at the other person's picture before actually committing to a relationship. They might have their reasons of course, but I, for one, feel that such a decision based largely on looks is more suitable for a casual relationship. It is bound to sizzle off after some time. After all, how long can you keep staring at a person? And what happens if the person doesn't stare back at you?

Or even worse, what happens if you find the person staring at another person? Looks may be important, but they certainly are not the most important thing and should never be used as the deciding factor if you are thinking about a serious relationship.

Common Interests

A human being is not like a piece of glass though which you can look and see the other side. A human being is more like a diamond, which when held against light reflects and deflects light so that a myriad of colors are seen. We're complex.

We have a lot of interest and the interests of one person need not match with the interests of another. But thankfully the interests are not as numerous as human beings. So we are bound to find a lot of people who share our interests. And if we can find someone like that, then our search should end there. So, what are your interests? That is something for you to find out.

Mind you, you might have to do some serious thinking before you level down you preferences. There might be a lot of things that you enjoy doing but about which you have given a second thought.

Your interests could be something like sports or outdoor activities. Or you could think of interests like social work or cross-words or religious interests. Keep the ball rolling; please understand that the words I have listed here are mere suggestions.

Your tastes and interests could be very different. So let them be. And once you have decided on what your interests are then half the story is done.

What Interests You In A Person?

This is probably the more important part of the story. Each one of us has to sit and think about what we would like in another person. Having the same interests doesn't necessarily mean that you can get along with a person.

For example, if you a person who likes to talk a lot, it doesn't mean that you could like another person who likes to talk a lot as well. If two people try to keep talking at the same time then obviously, there cannot be any dialogue.

So also, if you are the silent reserved type and the other person too is the silent reserved type, the there will hardly be any dialogue at all! The word over here is "compatible." The interests of partners should complement each other and not clash.

Keyword Searches

So now that you have decided what is it that interests you in a person and what your interests and tastes are, try such key word searches on a search engine like Google.

The idea over here is **not** to advertise yourself as a person who is in search of a life partner. No matter how well you put it, it looses that touch of subtlety once you are in a singles' chat room. So don't do it that way. You remember how we spoke about working backwards; this is how it is done.

We will tell you how to project yourself best in a later chapter but for now let us talk about finding Mr. Right or Ms. Right. An interesting thing to be noted here is that it is not difficult to fall in love with a person or to make a choice. The difficult part is to make the right choice and to fall in love with the right person.

Likes Versus Dislikes

The second thing that you could do is chalk out a list of qualities that you genuinely dislike in a person. Yes I am not joking! Dislikes are just as important, or even more important than likes. We all have to make compromises here and there, but if we start away by condoning things, which we genuinely dislike, it is going to tell on the relationship at sometime or the other.

I would like to give a word of caution over here. A lot of people make a mistake when they are courting. They put up their best behavior, which is very good of course, but they try to be very adjusting and accommodating which is NOT very good. A point that they tend to over look is that they are not going to be going on a camping trip with this person that they are trying to impress; they are going to be living the rest of their lives with the person.

So it is best not to be very *"oh so very accommodating and adjusting."*

You can afford to stick to things that you are very particular about. And if you have any thoughts that you will be able to mold the person out of his or her offending habits at a later date, forget it.

The moment you start trying to mold or cajole the person out of his or her habits, whatever they may be, the word becomes 'nagging' and if at all the person does drop the habit, he or she will love you less for it.

It really **doesn't** work that way. So it's best to have a clear idea about qualities and habits that you genuinely dislike in a person and steer clear of the 'lesser mortals' who have those habits.

Once you have a fairly clear idea about your likes and dislikes you are in a better position to make the right choice. And considering the multitude of people out there, you do not have to worry or be over anxious that you just might not find any one at all. He or she is out there, and if you are doing what you are doing right, namely barking up the right tree you will succeed.

There are some people who even believe that every thing is ordained. It has been written down who should marry who and in the end only that which should happen will happen. Well, I don't know about that, but I do know that dating helps speed up the process.

Another thing that you could do is that you could just let nature take its course. Oh nature has its wonderful ways. There is a lot of chemistry involved in the selection of partner so maybe the best thing we could do is lend nature a helping hand.

Friends First

Try to look at this endeavor not as a prospective husband/wife hunt but as an effort to make a lot of friends, and I mean good friends. Friends that you can laugh aloud with, friends who make you laugh. Not everyone can make us laugh, and when I say laugh, I am not referring to some comedian. We are talking about friends here.

It really does pay to have a lot of friends. It makes ones life richer. The best thing about friends is that you can be yourself with them. And they too can be themselves with you. And that means letting it all out. We must remember that apart from being the dutiful husband or wife, your spouse should be your best friend as well.

That is one mistake that most couples make. They tend to look upon their friends and their spouses as separate. While it is perfectly ok to have your own friends, your best friend should always be your husband or wife.

It should be someone you can share your dreams and fears with, someone who understands, someone who can give your hand a gentle squeeze when things go wrong and someone who can brighten up your darkest day.

All this is a very far cry from sex right? That is why we did mention earlier that looks and sex should be the last criteria in the selection of a life partner. The marriage proposal must come as a natural sequence and it should by no means be the first thing that comes out as soon as you warm up to a person. You cannot very well say something like, *"hey, you know what, I think we have the same tastes so let's get married."*

You can say that of course but it would not be in very good taste. So what do you do if you discover that one of the friends that you made and the one who you were keeping your fingers crossed about is already married?

Do you have a car? Then the answer is simple, just run over that person's spouse and remove the unwanted element, right? Wrong! It is just not done. You can still be friends with that person and shift your attention towards another direction. Who knows, you might even find a better person. All you have to do is shuffle your cards and deal them out again.

I hope you have got the hang of what we meant by working backwards now? Good. There is another catch involved in this process. There is a chance that one of the friends that you made may have read this book too and maybe the proposal may come from the other end.

If it does, then well and good; for it saves you the ritual.

Mr. Right and Ms. Wrong

But then, what if the **person who proposes to you wasn't really what you had in mind**? Well, the choice is yours of course; you can take it or leave it. But there is a point worth considering over here. If we can find someone that we love that is good, but if we find some one who **loves us, isn't that better?**

But I would also like to add a word over here. Suppose some one does come and propose to you but unfortunately, you are not in the least interested? You have every right to turn the proposal down but please do it gracefully. There is no need to hurt the other person's ego. This person is obviously a friend of yours, and surely you care deeply for them. However, if you know that you cannot marry this person, a turned-down proposal is better than a divorce.

Try to explain your feelings in the gentlest way possible.

Step 2: Making Yourself Look Like A Million Dollars

Nobody is perfect in this world but that does not mean that we cannot try to look our best. There is absolutely nothing wrong in giving nature a helping hand. Work on your image, work on your profile, and work on your appearance.

Many people go by the philosophy, *"this is me, whether you like it or not it's your problem. I am not going to change."* Well, nobody is asking you to change, but what are you trying to do? Scare people off?

Well, the fact is, such statements are just a manifestation of your own insecurity. We all have a certain degree of insecurity, some people more than others. It is this insecurity that makes us sound gruff and uncaring when it comes to improving our appearances.

Come on, what are you afraid of? I'll give you a tip. Whatever you are afraid of, others are afraid of the same thing. In this world, most people are neither for us nor against us. They are thinking about themselves.

Presenting oneself is an area that requires a lot of work, but surprisingly, this is the one area which people tend to neglect the most. Most of us have a laid back attitude when it comes to painting a picture about ourselves. When it comes to presenting yourself we really have some work to do.

If we knew you on a more personal basis we would have loved to help you to chalk out a profile of your self that would be as impressive as possible. But of course, it is impossible to know all our readers on a one to one basis.

But you do not have to worry because we have done a lot of study in this regard and once you follow our directions, you can indeed come up with that dream profile.

The Dream Profile

One cannot take too much effort in preparing a profile. It is something that should be viewed in all seriousness. Please do not treat the subject lightly. Imagine that you are preparing for a job; won't you spend a lot of time getting your resume ready?

Well, most of us take up jobs for how long, four or five years? And how about a relationship, definitely we do not embark on a relationship with the expectation that it would last for just a couple of years.

We have to understand that a relationship is really worth much more than a job, because it is probably the most important decision in your life. So now let us discuss ways in which you can spruce up your profile.

You can of course get a professional to do the job for you since it saves you the effort. You may have to dish out a small amount of course, but it could be worth it. There are many people who have qualms about including a picture in the profile. Well, I don't want to press the issue. It certainly does look better to have a picture in your profile, but due to privacy issues you can refrain from including a picture.

The best thing you could do is once you are comfortable chatting with a person and are convinced that this person does not have any devious intentions, you could send your picture over as an attachment or a file. But this, too, is best done a mutual exchange basis. It would be unfair if you know what the other person looks like but the other person is kept in the dark and vice versa.

The Face In The Mirror

Now, coming to the picture as such, if you are sending over a picture of yourself, for heavens sake, send over a decent picture. It should be a recent one and please do not make any compromises about the quality. Get a professional to do the job for you and with the digital techniques of today, they can do a very impressive job.

At the same time do work on your expression before the photograph is taken. Stand in front of your mirror and try out various expressions till you get something that you think is the best for you. And remember that it has to be a picture of you smiling. You should not have the classic hang dog expression, or the "*butter-will-not-melt-in-my-mouth expression*". Smile, it costs you nothing and it really lights up a person's face.

Now, the first thing that you should do is take out a pencil and paper and write down the raw details about yourself. By raw details we are referring to things like you age, your height and your weight.

This is the skeleton of which we are going to work on. And when we have added enough flesh and blood to this backbone, why even you will be impressed by your profile! But first let us steer clear of certain pit falls into which most people fall.

The Modesty Pitfall

Most of us have been trained to be very modest. When it comes to saying something good about our selves we feel very queasy about blowing our own trumpet. Right, no body is asking you to do any trumpet blowing but facts have to be stated as facts.

If you are a music lover and have a good voice too, I can't see why you can't put it down like that itself. Why can't you declare simply without sounding very proud that you have good voice? A pointer that you could bear in mind would be to add something like, "My friends think that I sing rather well."

There now, you can't feel too bad about something as simple as that. It is as good as saying "*some people think that I sing well, but it is for you to decide whether I have a good voice or not.*" Similar statements that you can work on and even add are given below.

- "*Lots of people appreciate my cooking.*"
- "*I am no Rembrandt, but I enjoy painting.*"
- "*I like decorating, and many of my friends think that my tastes are not too bad.*"

So go ahead, if you really have a talent, you might as well as let others know about it, after all a talented person would any way like to be appreciated by a partner.

While we are talking about modesty, there is one question that I want to address right now. It is something that all of us are familiar with. If you have chatted with a stranger with whom you are trying to build a rapport you must have been confronted with the question before. The question is "what do you look like?'

I have often wondered about the sense of this question. The best answers that I could come up with are "I look like a cross between an orangutan and a Tasmanian devil" or "I have my mothers teeth, my fathers nose, my uncle's eyes and my roommates' shoes."

But of course we cannot give such answers which funny though they might sound, might just rub the person in the wrong way. What the person actually means is, "are you good looking or not?"

A very tricky question indeed! How can you answer such a question with out sounding either super modest or extremely vain? The answer to that is not to tell them the answer directly. You can say something like:

- "*I am as fresh as peppermint.*"
- "*I look like a bunch of fresh lilies.*"
- "*I have the appeal of a bowl of fresh fruit.*"

If the person still does not take the hint, then give them a detailed description of ever inch and let he or she decide for himself or herself.

The Braggart Pitfall

Bragging, as we all know, is a major turnoff. So it is best to steer completely clear of it. This is especially true in the case of physical attributes. You might be one hell of a looker, but let the other person decide, remember that what wine is for Peter can turn of to be venom for Paul.

You can make implied statements like, "*I am certainly not a bad looker,*" or "*opinion is divided, some people think that I am good looking while others think that I am not.*" But perhaps the best way of describing yourself would be to add a touch of humor to it.

If you are chubby you could say something like, "*I am round in all the right places…I hope.*" If you are tall you could say something like, "*some say I should play basketball.*" If you are on the short side you could say something like, "*I might seem to lacking in size but I assure you, it is all there.*"

You know what is the best part about such witty remarks about oneself? Humor always works. All of us have been blessed with a sense of humor to some degree at least and if a person is able to make funny comments about himself or herself, that always acts as a turn on. And you can take my word for it; humor sells like a billion dollars.

The Hackneyed Pitfall

We have seen and heard other people describe themselves and these kind of descriptions sort of sink into our heads. The moment some one asks us to describe ourselves, we start off by using such hackneyed phrases.

I think it is much better to completely steer clear of hackneyed phrases. It makes us look like just another face in the crowd. Tell me, unless you have an identical twin, have you ever seen any one who looks exactly like you?

Then why on earth should your description of yourself sound like a banal organ that has been played again and again. Try to sound as original as you can. Make yourself sound interesting.

Try to use as many similes and comparisons as possible. If you are blonde, well don't just say that you are blonde. You could descriptions like, "*My hair is the color of freshly harvested hay.*"

If you are a brunette you could say something like:

> "*My hair color would make a raven blush.*" *If you have red hair, you could try something like,* "*My hair is like the setting sun.*"

Another point that I would like to add is you do not have to belittle yourself. Every coin has two sides and it all depends on the way you look at it. For example, if you have dark skin, there is absolutely no reason to feel bad about it. It all depends on how you put it across. You could try expressions like, "*If you like chocolate then you are going to love the color of my skin.*" Or "*My body looks like polished wood.*"

Remember, beauty lies in the eyes of the beholder, and it is left to you to convince the beholder. Most people are willing to believe what you tell them, provided you tell them convincingly enough.

The Boredom Pitfall

Try to make yourself sound as interesting as possible. I mean it. If you are painting a self portrait you might as well use the right colors. Before we leave our homes what do we do? We all spend at least five minutes in front of our mirrors in an attempt to make our selves look as presentable and as impressive as possible.

Well, the same thing applies to our profile. Remove all drab details about yourself that might be of no interest to the reader. If you job is something like *editing journals on the etymology of words derived from ancient Aramaic*, well, just say that you have an editing job.

Similarly try to bear in mind that anything can be put down in two ways. You can either make it interesting or boring; so work on it until you are sure that it will not bore a reader to death and the best test for this would be to hand it over to a close friend and ask that friend's opinion. Nobody likes a bore so take all efforts not to sound like one.

The Vagueness Pitfall

At the same time what ever you put down about yourself must not be confusing. It just does not work to put down a statement like, "*while I am not really given to sports, nor am I considered to be an outdoor person, I have developed a passing interest in watching football, and have had my stints with Terra firma.*"

Phew! If, anything drives people away, statements like this certainly do. For Heaven's sake avoid phrases like "*I am different,*" especially when you are talking about your appearance. The other person will in all likelihood conjure up images of a three horned monster or a lion tailed monkey.

Another example is when you use phrases like, "*I don't play by the rules*," or "*I am game for something new.*" These expressions can be hopelessly misleading and it is the easiest thing in the world to add a sexual innuendo to such an expression and that would be a sure shot method of biting off more than you can chew.

Now that we have discussed the major pitfalls, let us go the real profile. The reason I said real profile is that the profile must indeed reflect the person you are.

The Web of Deceit

While you might take some care to conceal your identity it is best **not to lie**.

Do not try to bluff your way through a relationship because at sometime the whole thing might come out and as we all know, one lie leads to another and then before you know it the whole relationship will crash. Be as honest and as frank as you can, taking care to conceal your identity.

Some one once said that a friend is some one who knows all about you and loves you just the same. So there is no need to hide things about you. Of course you do not have to tell the person every ghastly, gory detail about yourself, but at the same time you do not have to conjure up stuff about you that just is not true.

If at all you do paint a very rosy picture about yourself, including things that just are not true, or are far-fetched exaggerations, and the other person does flip for you, in reality you will be basking in another person's glory. This picture you have painted is just not you.

Your Alter Ego

When you choose a handle to identify yourself by, you have to be sharp. Do not try to attract as many partners as possible. After all, what are we looking for, quality or quantity? Try to attract only the kind of people you are interested in and who would find you interesting.

That is why we suggested that you use a handle that better defines the kind of person you are. Do not try to sound like a sex god or a sex goddess. If you are, let the other person decide for him self or her self; (it is much better than having the person come up with statements like "*is it in yet?*") So steer clear of handles like Megastud, Handsomehunk, Superbabe or Bedlover.

Instead of that you could try handles that gives one an immediate idea about the kind of person you are. If you are an outdoor person use something like Natureguy or Naturegirl; if you are a music freak use something like Musicman or Musicmaid. If you are into theatre and stuff like that you could choose a name like Theatreguy or Theatregirl.

The point is to win over people who are interested in the same stuff as you are. That of course increases your chances of gelling with the person.

Brevity is Key

Another crucial thing about writing your profile is that you should keep it as brief as possible. Nobody and that means nobody wants to read through lines and lines of another person's profile. If you make it so long winded the person who is reading it will get the idea that you are the kind of person who would love to keep on talking about yourself and instead of go on a date with you, the reader would rather curl up and die.

But that doesn't mean that you have to limit the whole thing to just a few words. A too brief profile would sound as if you do not have time for all this, but you are just doing it for the heck of it.

The best style that you could use would be to be 100% natural. Write your profile as you would describe yourself to a person directly. The conversation style has the widest appeal I might add. Make it simple and stay away from big words and hackneyed expressions.

You are Unique

Think about it for a minute. Look at yourself in the mirror. Do you look like anyone else that you know? We all look so different though essentially we have been endowed with the same external characteristics, which are one nose, one mouth, two eyes and two ears.

So in spite of having the same building blocks, if we can look so different why do we have to sound alike? Think about yourself in a different way. Do not just consider your likes and dislikes when you are writing your profile, consider your endearing qualities as well. Endearing qualities, what are those?

Those are those qualities which make you liked by others. Of course, these are things that we never bother, about but maybe we should. So what I would suggest would be to ask your best friends why they like you. Who knows, their answers just might surprise you! But at least you will get an idea of what you can include in your profile.

You could try out the following exercise to find out what kind of a person you are. I won't say that the results are absolutely fool proof but they certainly might be interesting.

The Animal Test

Which among the following animals do you identify with most?

- A shark
- A rabbit
- A bear
- A hen
- A dog and finally
- A cat

- If you chose a **shark**, you are generally an aggressive kind of person who has no time for others who are not up to the mark. You won't think twice about slicing through those who stand in your way and you have a very clear idea about what you want and you know how to get it too.

- If you chose a **rabbit** you are generally sweet tempered but timid. You bend very easily. You like to stay clear from the limelight as far as possible and do not interfere much in the affairs of others.

- If you chose the **bear**, you are a warm person by nature but not very sure about whether others like you. Hence you might go out of your way to win friends and love reassuring others.

- If you chose the **hen**, then you are one of those people who constantly fuss about minor details. You keep your eyes open but you are very dependable though sometimes you might end up poking your nose into things that do not concern you.

- If you chose the **dog** you are a happy go lucky person. You are willing to help others but if you do not watch out, more than once you might be taken for a ride. You do not bother about trifles but when you lose your head, it is really lost.

- Hmm, you chose the **cat** did you? Well you live in a world of your own; you do not trouble others and do not like others troubling you. In short you are very much the modern apartment creature who knows all the manners but uses them only to be civil.

Now, the descriptions given here are just general guidelines but I suppose that it does give you a cue about how to write your own profile. You can do it by yourself. Think about the animal or bird that you like best. Do not consider physical attributes but think of traits or characteristics that you like.

Then you can sit down and write a brief description about the animal and hey presto! Before you even know it, your profile is ready but it would be a good idea to delete the name of the animal when you post your profile.

There is something that I want all my readers to understand. Each one of us has something remarkable about us. It is all a question of finding out what those qualities are. **Do not always believe what other people have to say about you.** Don't you have something to say about yourself?

Pretend as if you were talking to your best friend. Talk to yourself. If your best friend **were to ask you what his or her endearing qualities are then wouldn't you be quick to** reassure the person? Well, the same thing applies to you as well. You can be your own best friend. And when you try out this exercise on yourself, well, you have a list of your plus points ready. Common if you can do this to your friend, then you can do it to yourself as well.

Such an exercise is very useful not just from the dating point of view but only if we understand what are our positive traits are, can we understand what kind of a person we deserve to get. The same holds true about our negative traits too, but then nobody is perfect.

Step 3: Letting The Relationship Blossom

Right, so now we are as ready as we can be with our interests all chalked out and our profiles posted. It is perfect picture. It is almost like being seated alone at this posh restaurant, dressed to kill, with a glass of champagne in one hand and the other hand swung over the back of the chair. You have a smile on your lips, a twinkle in your eye and an invitation on your face.

So what happens next? This person who appears to be the perfect match for you catches your eye and saunters towards you. Now what do you do? Please remember that the description above was pertaining to a virtual environment. In effect, what we meant is that while you spend time idling in a chat room, this is the mood that you are going to generate.

So what happens when a person takes the cue and starts chatting? Well, that really is an intelligent question. I would like to make one thing straight over here. The Internet is like any other highway. It is not safe until you get to know your way around. So what I would suggest would be to trust your instincts and proceed with caution. You can sound like a very warm person but please be extremely cautious about giving out any personal information.

Nicknames and Pet names

Let the other person know that you would prefer to be known by the handle you use or even better, you could tell the person to call you a pet name but let the person know that it is indeed a pet name, because at a later date, if the relationship really blossoms it doesn't look nice if you have to say something like, *"Gee, I'm sorry, but my name isn't really Janice, it is Heptullah, I guess I lied to you."*

The best thing in this case would be to let your self be known by the name of some celebrity. You could call yourself Cinderella or Pocahontas or Archie, or Betty or Veronica. The chatting has now begun and you can start exchanging information. Keep to the general and stay away from the specific.

Helping your Memory

The human brain is indeed a remarkable thing. It is capable of storing and processing such a wide range of information that even a supercomputer would shy away when compared to it. But due to the virtual explosion of information, our memories have become very selective.

This means that we cannot recollect everything that we hear or see. Do not trust your memory too much when it comes to chatting over the net. You might meet a lot of people over the net and you might chat with a couple of them. So eventually it might become difficult to remember all of them and their details as well.

Or even worse than that is that you might become confused and mix up details. It would look bad for you if you call a person the wrong name, or ask the person the wrong details. In such cases where you have been chatting with a number of persons, for heaven's sake jot down the details about each person separately or create separate files for each person ad store them in your computer.

When you add them to your friends list use handles or nicknames that can help you remember the person the moment you start chatting at a later date.

Now, in case you do not really remember the person, then it is unadvisable to play the guessing game. The other person might get very offended if you say something like, "Is it Sarah or Mary?"

In such cases when you have a genuine lapse of memory, the best thing to do is to be honest with the person and say, "I know we chatted the other day, but I'm terribly sorry, can you please refresh my memory about you?"

Small Talk

There are few topics that are best for the initial talks so that an intimacy is not developed and at the same time you do not have to struggle for matters of common interest. You can talk about the weather, sports, movies, music and even food.

But at the same it is in bad taste to discuss religion, politics and family matters in the initial stages. You can crack jokes but dirty jokes are an absolute no-no at least in the first few talks.

Once you have talked more than once or twice and you feel comfortable with the person you can give the person your e-mail address but remember this is the first step towards virtual intimacy so you have to trust your instincts and nothing else. This takes things out of the public chat rooms and into the private inboxes.

Beware of Instant Intimacy

There are many people who feel that e-mail will never have the warmth or the personal touch of the old-fashioned letters and cards that people used to send through the postal service. That may be true but e-mail has an advantage of the here and the now.

Because you are aware of the fact that the person you are chatting is reaching out to you in the same way as you are reaching out to that person, there is a tendency for an intimacy to build up even before you know it.

The medium ceases to be the deciding factor and when a person presses you for information which you have to supply immediately you might let certain details slip out unless you are well prepared.

You have to be on your guard all the time and keep constantly reminding your self that the person you are chatting with is, after all a stranger and a goodness-knows-what. The best thing that you could do is avoid instant intimacy altogether.

It doesn't really matter if the other person finds you cold or reserved, you can easily solve that by telling the other person that it takes sometime for you to become comfortable with a person. That in fact is a good quality because it is as good as saying, "Well, I'm sorry I'm not the loose kind who plays around."

There is something that many of my readers might want to know and that is how to find out if the other person is lying. As I had told you earlier, the Net can be a very unsafe place and so we have to be absolutely sure about the good faith of the other person before revealing any personal details about ourselves. So the next part has been devoted specifically for that.

4 Ways To Tell If Someone Is Lying

1. As discussed earlier, we are not going to resort to singles' chat rooms dedicated specifically to online dating. Instead we will be in chat rooms of specific interest. So one very effective way of finding out if a person is lying would be to **ask the person very pointed questions about the area of interest**. If the person fumbles or gives vague answers then you do not have to waste your time on such a person.

2. Another thing that you could do is that from the moment you first make contact, jot down whatever details the person chooses to reveal to you and in subsequent encounters nonchalantly question the person about the details, **if there is a contradiction in the two details** then you can be as sure as pat that the person is lying.

3. **Ask the person seemingly general questions but which in fact should have a very definite purpose**, for example ask the person what he or she is looking for in such a relationship. Note down the answer. After two or three encounters again repeat the question and see whether the two answers match.

4. **You could try pretending that you have chatted with the person before and innocently ask the person if he or she is such and such person (make something up) and try offering compliments** to the person like, "I really enjoyed chatting with you the other day. You were perfectly charming…" and so on. If the person falls for cheap flattery like this, then obviously he or she makes it a hobby to chat with people under various identities.

And so the chatting goes on until the person really grows on you. When you feel that you can really trust the person, you may try giving the person your telephone number. Remember that this too is a giant leap towards building a relationship so it's better that you be sure than sorry.

The safest thing you can do about telephone numbers is to mutually exchange it **preferably at the same time, so that neither party is at a disadvantage.** It's really no big deal, you can afford to tell the person that you are just being wary, the person will understand. If he or she does not, then there is a good chance that he or she will not understand a lot of other things as well. In that case, dump the person.

Step 4: Meeting Face To Face

Once you have started talking over the telephone, then the relationship has already taken wings, then is no reason to postpone a direct meeting. So what are we waiting for? But wait; there is no need to push it. You should not sound over anxious to meet this girl or guy.

Let the decision to meet evolve over a number of telephone calls. And there are certain things that you can bear in mind before you really meet.

The Rendezvous

It is not advisable to invite someone home before you have really met the person. You had better choose a public place preferably somewhere where there are plenty of people around, just in case, you know.

That is why most couples prefer to meet in a restaurant over lunch or dinner. There is one thing about having food together. When people sit together and have food together they get to know a lot about each other.

Table manners tell us a lot about a person's upbringing and background and you can learn a lot about a person by observing him or her eat. The second thing is that warm food has a wonderful effect on the human mind. It releases all those digestive juices and sets the tongue wagging. People loosen up a lot, especially after a glass of wine or two.

The first mistake that most people make is that they go under the wrong impression that a meeting, even the first meeting must end up in bed. No, it does not have to be so.

There is no compulsion on your part or anyone's part that you have to take the person home with you. Just because you enjoy talking or chatting with a person it does not necessarily mean that you have to sleep with the person. Let that too evolve, so it is best to keep any such situations that might lead to a bed room scene completely at bay.

So how do you do that? The first thing you should do is that you should be clear about the time. Evenings are tricky times to meet. If you have dinner together, then there comes the possibility of dropping the other person home.

And of course you can't just accept a ride and walk away after being dropped without inviting the other person in. And then one thing will lead to the other and then the inevitable is bound to happen. Of course, if that's the way you would like it to be then you just have to do what I just told you not to do.

Lunch time is the best time because in the day time most of us are busy with work and we can just spare an hour or a half for lunch. So you can always leave on the pretext that you have to get back to work or something like that. Very few people end up going home together after lunch. Another thing is that at lunch the element of romance does not really come in.

Take care to be at the arranged spot on time, you certainly do not want to keep a person you are meeting for the first time waiting. Dress appropriately for the occasion, keep it simple but at the same time it should be something that looks good on you.

Leaving Your Mark Behind

Now, suppose this date did work out as planned and you really and thoroughly enjoyed the company of the other person you would want the other person to remember you and think about you, wouldn't you? So how do you make sure that the other person does think about you?

The answer is simple. Just leave your mark behind. Mind you, a business or visiting card is not appropriate here. It lends a very formal color to the picture. Surely you do not want the person to remember you for your credentials or your designation. Something more personalized would be more appropriate.

Put your artistic and creative talents into full gear. If you are poetic, you could pen down a few lines on a small card and hand it to the person. Mind you, the lines should not be about the person, but about general topics like friendship, relationships, togetherness, warmth, or meetings. But do the writing in advance and keep it for the right moment. Do not try to write a poem on a paper napkin with the person sitting in front of you!

If you can't write poetry, maybe you could get some dried flowers and stick them onto a card and copy down the lines of somebody else, but admit that the lines are not your to the person.

Keep such a token with you and wait for the right moment. Just before you part, if you are sure that *"this is the one"* then hand it over to the person with a very shy expression on your face and a timid, "*I made this for you…*" Believe me, it's miles better to say "I made this for you" than "*I bought this for you*".

So what happens if you are not too sure that you want to see this person again? Well keep it with you itself and save it for the next person.

If the person is the right person, and if you did hand the person this personalized token, the person is sure to think of you in a much fonder way.

Clothes Maketh A Man (Or Woman)

You do not have to be dressed to kill when you go out to lunch. The best thing about lunch dates is that most of would be in our work clothes and that saves us the agony of choosing the right thing to wear on a first date.

A wonderful thing that you could do when going on a fist date is to make it a group activity, preferably a foursome. This takes away the awkwardness of the situation and definitely takes away all those embarrassing moments of silence.

A group has another advantage in that lesser attention will be focused on each other so that there is less stress and as a result both partners would be more relaxed. It is also safer too, since there is safety in numbers.

But the company to be included should be mutually agreeable and not be thrust upon the other person. But take care to avoid any person who you know to be a chatterbox; it takes all the fun away if one person dominates the conversation.

You may drink if you want to, but do not drink too much on your first date. Not only is it in bad taste but when you are drunk, you might blurt out something which you didn't mean to and that might ruin every thing.

Footing the Bill

It is a good idea to decide before hand and communicate your decision to go Dutch, which means that each person should pay for whatever he or she has. That's the way that it is supposed to be because if nothing works out of this relation you certainly do not want to be obliged to the person.

When you choose the place, avoid secluded spots and places that you are not familiar with. But the ambience is indeed important. You cannot expect to have a tête-à-tête in a crowded shopping mall, can you? I think that is about it about your first date.

Many Dates

So what happens if you get more than one offer to date at more or less the same time? Or in other words, what happens if you become close to more than one person at a time? Hey, that is probably the very thing we are looking out for. You could go on different dates and then compare for your self and choose the best person.

You do not have to leap for the first person who caught your fancy. You have the right to choose, so go ahead and do it. There is no need to feel guilty about two timing any body as long as you do not promise any one that you are not seeing any one else.

And what happens if you bump into date number one while you are out with date number 2. Well, all you have to do is treat it as the most natural thing in the world. Introduce date No.1 to date No.2 as your friends and watch how they behave. This is an excellent way of finding out how a jealous husband or wife may behave in future.

But what ever happens, a double date, that is going out with two people together is completely out of the question!

Offline Dating: How To Make That Great Impression

When you are dating online, you have a lot of things to your advantage. For example, the other person does not really see you and you do not really have to bother about appearances. You can devote your entire energy towards sounding intelligent and witty.

But when you are actually seated in front of a person, there are a thousand things that you have to pay attention to. There are many people who believe that it is not really important to keep up appearances. They feel that it is more important to be oneself.

It sounds good enough. But on your first date at least you certainly have to keep up appearances. The other person should not feel ashamed to be seen around with you and so you should try as hard as possible to avoid that faux pas.

Let us start with your physical appearance. While I did mention earlier that you do not have to be dressed to kill, it is very important that you have to appear well groomed. Take special care about things like nails, hair, and teeth. Check for bad breath too because that indeed is the worst turn off.

What you wear should not be loud and attract the wrong kind of attention. Choose something that you are comfortable in and at the same time that looks good on you. Ladies, please be careful about your make-up, and remember that make-up is meant to accentuate your looks not to hide it. It is best to avoid garish colors.

You should smell good of course but don't over do it. We certainly don't want you to remain in the other person's memory as just one strong smell. Men, please take care to go in for masculine scents like musk, or smells from nature. Women, keep it as light and dainty as possible.

The Secret is Charm

All the things that have been said so far are about how you can create a favorable impression. There is something that is equally or even more important than that, and that is to make the other person feel comfortable. Help the other person relax.

Any way you have been chatting for quite some time so you do know a great deal about each other. The best thing you can do is to ease the tension and break the ice. Sometimes the ice gets so thick that you can literally feel it. Break it up by cracking a joke or two.

But the joke should be spontaneous and in keeping with the situation or else it will fall flat. Do not rehearse a joke because a rehearsed joke sounds…well…rehearsed.

The key word here is charm. Use all the charm that you can muster. Try to be as considerate and as thoughtful as possible. Do not dominate the conversation but try to get the other person talking. People generally love to talk about themselves so try to get the other person talking by asking about the person's work. Show interest in whatever the other person says.

Try to be a good conversationalist. A good conversationalist is not a person who talks well, but is one who listens well as well. So try to be a good listener. And while you are listening try not to get distracted by something else or the other person might feel that you are losing interest in what he or she is saying.

Then comes the question, "what do you do if you find that the other person is dominating the conversation?"

Well, in that case listen patiently for a minute or two and then give a subtle sign like a raised eyebrow or a smile through the corner of your mouth. If the other person is intelligent enough, he or she will get the cue. If not, then take your chance, you might have to listen to this person for the rest of your life.

Humor rarely fails. But again take care not to over do it. There is only one thing worse than a total lack of humor and that is too much humor.

Gifts?

It is a good idea to take a gift along with you as that does create a good impression, but remember that when you are courting the gifts should be limited to flowers or chocolates only. While you are chatting try to find out what the other person likes in flowers and chocolates. You certainly don't want to give the person flowers that he or she is allergic to.

The object of your gift should not be to woo the person but to create a good and lasting impression. There is no sense in splurging a lot on your first date for there is no rule that every thing should work out well the first time itself. Do not over do it and at the same time do not appear cheap and stingy either.

However if the other person has forgotten to bring you a gift, be quick to reassure the person that it is perfectly alright. Do not let the other person feel uneasy. In fact, that is a wonderful way to make the conversation light. You can jokingly tell the other person to get you a gift the next time.

Step 5: Once Bitten…

Many of my readers might be worried that everything does not work out like has been described, what would they do? Or in other words if this first date does not work out what should they do?

The answer is very simple, repeat the whole process again!

Let's go back to where we started. Remember, this is a chance to find the partner for life so we might have to grow many plants before we get the right harvest.

I am not talking about two timing here. What I mean is that instead of putting all your eggs in one basket, keep the avenues open. **Don't just bank on one person, because if that doesn't work out, you might lose heart.** You can hope for the best but expect the contrary as well.

Only the every lucky ones get the right pick at the first go it self. For the rest of us, we just have to keep trying till we succeed. Another advantage of trying out different people is that you can get to choose. It should not be that you just flipped for the first guy or girl who came your way. Take you time, give yourself some breathing space and then make the right decision.

Nobody can force you into making a commitment. It should be completely your choice. Of course, if you get the right cues and something deep down inside tells you that this is the right person for you, then what are you waiting for, go ahead and show the green signal.

But on the other hand if someone is trying to force you into making a commitment and you feel hard pressed, gently try to break away. All you have to do is put your foot down very firmly and tell the person that you need more time.

However, it is not good to keep a person waiting indefinitely. Tell the person that you **need perhaps a week's time or more than that. But don't let the person realize that you** are checking out other people. Just tell them that this is probably the most important decision in your life so you just want to be sure.

In Closing...

I would like to add one word about signing off. In case things do not work out please take care to part gracefully. In such instances it is not the best decision to say such things over chat. The other person may put forward some very uncomfortable questions that you will have a tough time answering.

The best thing you cold do is send the person an e-mail telling him or her that he or she was not really what you had in mind, but you would like to remain good friends all the same.

You do not have to worry about being pestered by the other person in future; the "good friends" part never fails. Most people dislike to be called a good friend after a close encounter. In most cases the relationship just sizzles out after this. However please remember that it is indeed bad manners to part with out a word and just stop answering mails without any information at all.

Some people do that because they do not want to offend the other person. But such callousness is really worse.

So that is all about it. You know everything that is to be known and **the ball is now well and truly in your courts.** So what are you waiting for, why don't you go out there and make your presence felt and come back with the catch of a lifetime.

I don't think that we have left any stones unturned and from here I'm sure that on your first date everything will be well in your control.

To your first dating success online!

www.ingramcontent.com/pod-product-compliance
Ingram Content Group UK Ltd.
Pitfield, Milton Keynes, MK11 3LW, UK
UKHW022218230426
12048UKWH00016BA/914